C000003588

GREEK MYTH PLAYS

10 **READERS THEATER** SCRIPTS BASED ON FAVORITE GREEK MYTHS
THAT STUDENTS CAN READ AND REREAD TO DEVELOP THEIR FLUENCY

NEW YORK • TORONTO • LONDON • AUCKLAND • SYDNEY
MEXICO CITY • NEW DELHI • HONG KONG • BUENOS AIRES

Teaching
Resources

Scholastic Inc. grants teachers permission to photocopy the plays from this book for classroom use. No other part of this publication may be reproduced in whole or in part, or stored in a retrieval system, or transmitted in any form or by any means, electronic, mechanical, photocopying, recording, or otherwise, without written permission of the publisher. For information regarding permission, write to Scholastic Inc., 557 Broadway, New York, NY 10012.

Editor: Maria L. Chang
Cover design by Ka-Yeon Kim
Cover photograph by Getty Images © Wilfried Krecichwost
Interior design by Grafica, Inc.
Interior illustrations by George Ulrich

ISBN-13: 978-0-439-64014-5
ISBN-10: 0-439-64014-8
Copyright © 2008 by Carol Pugliano-Martin
All rights reserved.
Printed in the U.S.A.

4 5 6 7 8 9 10   40   15 14 13 12 11 10

TABLE OF CONTENTS

INTRODUCTION

A few years ago, I taught a mythology unit to a class of third graders. The unit lasted for several months, and from beginning to end all of my students were thoroughly engaged. I was really amazed at how their enthusiasm for the unit never wavered. They actually hated to see it end! During the unit, we performed some plays and, while we enjoyed those that we did, I wished there was another book of plays for us to do. Thus, the idea for this book was born.

BUILDING FLUENCY THROUGH READERS THEATER

Plays may seem frivolous at first glance, but they actually perform an important role in the language arts curriculum. Readers Theater, in particular, has been proven time and again to help boost fluency and comprehension, particularly in struggling readers (Martinez, Roser, and Strecker, 1999; Keehn, 2003). Fluency is a reader's ability to decode words quickly, accurately, and effortlessly. In its 2000 report, the National Reading Panel cited research that shows oral reading fluency is a critical factor in reading comprehension.

Picture a student who struggles reading a given text. As he stumbles to decode unfamiliar words, he puts much effort into trying to sound them out and pronounce them. By the time he reaches the end of the sentence, he has probably forgotten what he read at the beginning. Not much comprehension going on there. Now picture a student who can read fluently. She sails through the text, easily recognizing words and phrases at first sight. Rather than spending energy trying to decipher the words, she directs all her energy toward the more important task of making sense of the text—in other words, comprehending it.

So how does Readers Theater help create fluent readers? It gives readers a purpose, a reason to rehearse reading aloud with a focus on reading accurately as well as understanding and interpreting the text (Worthy and Broaddus, 2001). In

Readers Theater, students stand in front of an audience, usually their classmates, and read their parts directly from the script. There are hardly any costumes, props, or sceneries, so performers rely solely on their voices to bring the play to life. In order to have a successful performance, students need to "rehearse" or practice reading the script several times beforehand. And therein lies the key to fluency—repeated reading. This repeated reading practice increases fluency as well as comprehension, especially for struggling readers (Samuels, 1997). "With practice, the reader achieves fluency and can direct his or her attention toward making sense of the reading and away from the mechanics of decoding" (Rasinski, 2003).

The best part about Readers Theater is that it naturally motivates children to practice reading. When the purpose of reading is to perform in front of an audience, repeated reading becomes inherently interesting and engaging (Rasinski, 2003). Martinez, Roser, and Strecker (1999) studied two classrooms that used Readers Theater to increase children's oral reading fluency. At the end of the ten-week program, nearly all of the children made significant reading gains compared to similar classrooms that didn't participate in the program. One of the teachers, Ms. Carter, explained how Readers Theater helped her students: "The first is comprehension that results from having to become the characters and understand their feelings, and the second is the repetition and practice."

USING GREEK MYTHS IN READERS THEATER

In this book, you'll find ten Readers Theater scripts based on favorite Greek myths. (I deliberately stayed away from the more violent myths, as I feel they take away from any message they might be trying to convey.) Some of the myths show the Greeks' explanation for how something came to be; for example, the myth of Demeter and Persephone explains the changing seasons. Others teach a moral lesson. The story of Echo and Narcissus, for example, warns against vanity.

Instead of narrators, the plays in this book include two Chorus parts. In Greek theater, the Chorus helped the story along by narrating, commenting on the action, and interacting with the characters in the play. The same is true with the choruses in these plays. These parts can be played by one or more students to give everyone a chance to be part of the play.

To get the most benefit from each play, try these steps for a successful Readers Theater performance:

1. Consider presenting two or three plays per week so every student is part of a "repertory group." Introduce each new play on a Monday by reading it aloud to the class. This will help familiarize students with the story and characters. Be sure to read the different parts in such a way as to model good oral reading— an important way to build reading fluency in students (Rasinski, 2003). You may want to rehearse reading the play aloud to yourself beforehand, paying attention to phrasing, expression, and pacing.

2. After you finish reading the play, discuss the story with students. Go over the words in the glossary at the end of the play to ensure students understand unfamiliar words.

3. Hand out copies of the play to students. Allow students time to read over the script independently. In the meantime, decide how you want to group students, keeping in mind that "Readers Theater is an excellent activity for grouping students by interest rather than reading level" (Worthy and Broaddus, 2001). Consider giving each student two copies of the play—one to take home to practice with his or her family and one to keep in school for in-class rehearsals. Tell students in each repertory group that they will be giving a Readers Theater performance of the play on Friday.

4. On Tuesday and Wednesday, allot about 30–45 minutes for students to practice reading the play with their groups. Instead of assigning roles right away, encourage members of each group to switch roles at every reading of the play. This way, students get a feel for each character's lines and can start thinking about which role they would like to play. Don't worry about your more reticent students. When children read a part, they usually can step outside themselves and "become" a character. This helps alleviate the self-consciousness that can come with reading aloud in front of a group.

5. At the end of the session on Wednesday, assign roles so that at Thursday's rehearsal, students read only their assigned parts. It is very important that students take parts in which they can be successful (Worthy and Broaddus, 2001). The parts in each play vary in terms of how many lines each character has. More fluent readers can tackle larger parts, while those still trying to master reading can participate in smaller roles. Often a struggling reader will get so excited about playing a certain part, he or she may be willing to try a larger part the next time around. The confidence that can spring from such accomplishment is extremely rewarding to both student and teacher. After you've assigned roles, show students how to find their character's name on the script and highlight their lines so they can find their place easily.

6. On Thursday, allot about 30–45 minutes for students to rehearse their parts. Encourage them to read expressively and to prepare an entertaining presentation for their audience. If you want, allow children to prepare small props for their characters; for example, a simple crown for a king or queen. However, keep in mind that the main purpose of a Readers Theater is for students to use their voices to convey the story.

7. On Friday, set up the classroom to look like a theater or auditorium. Push the tables toward the back of the room and place chairs in rows, leaving room in front for the "stage." Consider inviting other classes, the principal, and even parents to be part of the audience. Students are sure to be even more excited and motivated to do their best.

A FEW FINAL WORDS

To supplement the scripts in this book, I've included tips for staging each play—in case your students' enthusiasm persuades you to go beyond Readers Theater and create a full-stage production of the play. You'll also find extension activities that cross other curriculum areas, such as science, math, and art.

However and whenever you use these plays, I hope you and your students will get as much out of reading and performing mythology plays as my former students did. It was an experience I hope they will never forget. I know I won't.

BIBLIOGRAPHY

Keehn, S. (2003). The effect of instruction and practice through Readers Theatre on young readers' oral reading fluency. *Reading Research and Instruction, 42*(4), 40–61.

Martinez, M. G., Roser, N. L., & Strecker, S. K. (1999). "I never thought I could be a star": A readers theater ticket to fluency. *The Reading Teacher, 54*(4), 326–335.

National Reading Panel. (2000). *Teaching children to read: An evidence-based assessment of scientific research literature on reading and its implications for reading instruction.* Bethesda, MD: National Institutes of Health.

Samuels, S. J. (1997). The method of repeated readings. *The Reading Teacher, 50*(5), 376–381.

Rasinski, T. V. (2003). *The fluent reader.* New York: Scholastic.

Worthy, J. & Broaddus, K. (2001). Fluency beyond the primary grades: From group performance to silent, independent reading. *The Reading Teacher, 55*(4), 334–343.

TIPS FOR PUTTING ON THE PLAYS

Readers Theater generally doesn't require stage sets, props, or costumes. However, if you would like to create a more elaborate production, here are a few suggestions:

THE GODS AND GODDESSES BAKE-OFF

When the gods and goddesses are summoned to Zeus, each god and goddess will need his or her own throne. As they enter, have each character carry his or her own chair. They can either set the chairs in a row, with Zeus and Hera in the middle, or in a semicircle. It may be helpful and humorous to have the actors wear large name labels that read: "Hello, My name is _____." For the cakes, you can have actors pantomime holding cakes. Or you can have each actor design his or her character's cake, either drawing it on paper or constructing it from cardboard. For example, Poseidon's cake can be in the shape of a fish or other sea creature, Dionysus's can have a bottle of wine or some grapes on top, Demeter's can have stalks of grain sticking out of it, and so on.

PANDORA'S BOX

The scene where the Miseries come out of the box can be performed in the following way: Get a box large enough to conceal a student crouching behind it. If possible, get a box with a flap on top that Pandora can open to one side and leave open as each Misery pops out. When Pandora and Epimetheus bring the box home, have them place it near the edge of the "stage." As the time comes for each Misery and Hope to come out of the box, have each actor come on stage one at a time and hide behind the box. One by one they pop up from behind the box and step in front to introduce themselves. The actors can either exit right after saying their line or wait until all have come out of the box and exit altogether. When Hope goes back in the box and as Pandora says good-bye, Pandora can close the flap of the box.

ECHO AND NARCISSUS

For the scene in which Narcissus gazes at himself in the pond, you might want to use a large mirror for the pond. If you can't get a mirror, try wrapping aluminum foil or Mylar® around a large piece of cardboard. Decide how to position the mirror so that the audience will be able to see Narcissus's reflection. You (or another student) might have to raise the mirror at an angle when Narcissus sees himself, and then lay the mirror flat when he tries to grab and kiss the image, so that his reflection can no longer be seen.

DEMETER AND PERSEPHONE

Several times during this play, the venue changes from Earth to the Underworld. You may want to change the scenery a bit to indicate this change. One way to do this would be to hang a light or brightly colored sheet behind the actors during the Earth scenes. Then change to a dark sheet during the Underworld scenes. Students may even want to paint the sheets with pictures to better show each place. For example, the Earth sheet could have flowers and a sun painted on it, and the Underworld could have creepy-looking ghosts, bare trees, rocks, and so on. Using clothespins, hang the sheets from a string that stretches across the stage area. An even simpler way of indicating scene changes would be to depict the two places on separate sheets of chart paper on a pad. Display the pad on an easel that's either off to the side or in the middle of the stage. When it comes time to change scenery, someone can simply flip the pad over and back for quick and easy changes.

ORPHEUS AND EURYDICE

As the lyre is such an integral part of this play, consider making one to use as a prop. Look for pictures on the Internet for reference. For the three-headed dog, Cerberus, have those actors simply stand close together to indicate that they are one creature. Or you can create a costume that would enclose all three. A relatively easy way would be to cut three holes in a sheet and have the children put the sheet over their heads through the holes. You can paint the sheet to look like a hairy beast. If you choose to go this route, make sure that Cerberus does not have to move much as you'll want to avoid the children falling as they walk closely together under the sheet.

ATHENA AND ARACHNE: HOW SPIDERS CAME TO BE

Students can either pantomime holding up tapestries for this play or make actual "tapestries" beforehand. One way is to draw the "woven" scenes on poster board—Athena's tapestry showing the "gods in all their glory" and Arachne's tapestry, which shows the gods looking silly. Leave a blank spot on both tapestries for the objects that the two women show customers. As Athena "weaves" the bird, for example, she can tape a picture of a bird on the blank spot on her tapestry. Arachne can do the same when she weaves her flower. Have the actors hold up the bird and flower alone for the audience to see before taping each piece to the large tapestry, without the audience seeing the finished work. When they are finished, the audience will see the bird and the flower incorporated into the god scenes on the completed "tapestries."

ATALANTA AND THE GREAT RACE

As you most likely won't have much room for running, the scene where Atalanta races Hippomenes can best be staged by having them run in place side-by-side. (You can either have them face the audience as they're "running" or have them placed diagonally so that the audience can see both characters). As Atalanta sprints ahead, she can simply move a bit ahead of Hippomenes even as they continue running in place. This will not only solve the space problem, it will also ensure that the audience can hear their lines, since they're not moving all around the stage. If you're using actual apples for props, you might want to have Hippomenes pantomime throwing them and then actually placing them on the ground near Atalanta. As she bends to pick up the apple at her feet, Hippomenes moves a bit ahead of Atalanta. If you'd rather not use props, simply have the actors pantomime the apples.

DAEDALUS AND ICARUS

The brief scene where Theseus is in the maze with the Minotaur can lend itself to some creative staging in your classroom. While Chorus 1 speaks the lines about Theseus trying to escape from the Minotaur, those two actors can wind their way through the rows of chairs in your classroom (or groups of chairs and desks, however your room is set up). This can give the audience a better sense of the maze than the traditional staging of actors performing up front.

KING MIDAS AND THE GOLDEN TOUCH

Toward the end of the play, Dionysus gives King Midas an amphora to fill with water and pour over everything he had turned to gold. An amphora (meaning "two-handled carrier" in Greek) was a pottery container used to store liquids like oil or wine. It usually had two handles, a swollen belly, narrow neck, and a large mouth, and was made of terracotta, a reddish-brown clay, decorated with black, brown, and white art. The art often depicted aspects of everyday life or featured scenes of important figures glorifying the gods and goddesses.

To create this prop, you can simply draw and color one on paper or make a more realistic one from clay or papier-mâché. Encourage your class to decide on an appropriate scene to be painted on the amphora, perhaps something depicting Dionysus, since he presents the amphora to Midas.

THE TROJAN HORSE

In the scene where the Greeks and Trojans go to war over Helen, it may be best to avoid prop swords and the like to ensure that no one gets hurt. Sometimes such props can also cause too much disruption in the play. One way to handle the war scene is to humorously have the actors pantomime boxing. There can be a lot of "fancy footwork," ducking missed punches, running away, and so on. Remind students that there should be no contact between the actors as even fake punches can sometimes hurt.

EXTENSION ACTIVITIES

THE GODS AND GODDESSES BAKE-OFF

Now your class can eat like the gods and goddesses with this quick and easy ambrosia recipe, which serves six. (*NOTE: Be sure to check for student allergies first!*) As a math challenge, have students calculate the necessary amounts needed to serve everyone in your class.

You'll Need:
- 1 can (20 oz.) chunk or crushed pineapple in juice or syrup
- 1 can (11 oz.) mandarin orange segments
- 1 1/2 cup seedless grapes
- 1 cup miniature marshmallows
- 1 cup flaked coconut
- 1 cup walnuts or pecans
- 3/4 cup sour cream
- 1 tablespoon sugar

To Do:
1) Drain pineapple and mandarin oranges.

2) Combine pineapple, oranges, grapes, marshmallows, coconut, and nuts in large bowl.

3) Mix sour cream and sugar together in a small bowl.

4) Stir the sour cream–sugar mixture into the fruit mixture.

5) Chill 1 to 2 hours and dig in!

PANDORA'S BOX

Invite students to write a short story from the point of view of one of the Miseries that Pandora let out of the box. What happened to this escapee after being freed? Where did it go? What did it do? Who did it affect? As an extension, encourage students to add Hope to their stories. What part can Hope play in order to help humans cope with this particular Misery? Invite students to share their stories with the class. You may even challenge them to turn their stories into Readers Theater plays, using themselves and/or other students as the characters to act out their stories.

ECHO AND NARCISSUS

Students are sure to be excited when they see the flower named after the character in this myth. Any time of year, you can force narcissus bulbs to grow in your classroom. You can even turn this flower-growing activity into a science experiment!

You'll Need:
- narcissus bulbs
- a shallow dish or bowl
- pebbles, gravel, or sand
- water
- flowerpot
- potting soil

To Do:

Add some gravel or sand to the shallow dish. Place two bulbs' roots (pointy side up) in the gravel. Add water. Next, put some potting soil in the flowerpot. Plant two more bulbs in the soil, not too deep, but deep enough to cover the bulbs. Water occasionally. Observe the growth over the next several weeks. In which type of container/environment did the bulbs grow best? You can also chart/graph the growth as it occurs. Keep watering the flowers and enjoy your narcissus blooms!

DEMETER AND PERSEPHONE

Persephone ate six pomegranate seeds and that sealed her fate. Explain to students that a pomegranate is a fruit, and that one way to tell if a particular produce is a fruit is if it has seeds. Bring in a variety of produce items, such as orange, tomato, bell pepper, carrot, asparagus, corn, and so on. Hold up the orange and ask students: "Is this a fruit?" Have students raise their hands if they think the orange is a fruit. Then hold up something a bit less obvious, like a tomato or a pepper. Ask them to vote on that as well. Then divide the class into small groups and distribute a variety of produce to each group. Encourage the groups to examine each item by either breaking it apart or cutting it open with a plastic knife and have them then determine which ones are fruits. Invite the groups to present their findings to the rest of the class. Did any of their perceptions change due to their observations? Some other produce that can make for interesting debates are peas, corn, broccoli, and asparagus.

ORPHEUS AND EURYDICE

The story of Orpheus and Eurydice was made into an opera in the 1700s with music by Christoph Willibald Gluck. You may want to borrow a copy of the opera from the library as an introduction to this activity. (The Italian title is *Orfeo ed Euridice*.) After students have listened for a bit, invite them to write their own songs for their own opera about the myth. Start by listing the different scenes from the story that would make good songs. Some examples are when Orpheus finds out about what happened to Eurydice, when Orpheus is pleading with Hades to let Eurydice come home with him, and when Orpheus looks back to Eurydice and loses her forever. Then divide the class into groups, one for each scene you have written on the board. Assign each group a scene and invite students to write a song for their scene. Encourage the groups to put their songs to music and perform for the class. You can put them all together and tell the entire story through song, just like a real opera!

ATHENA AND ARACHNE

Are your students brave enough to challenge Athena with their own weaving? They can test their skills with this simple weaving activity.

You'll Need:
* shirt cardboard or a placemat-sized piece of cardboard (one for each child)
* ruler
* pencil
* twine
* a variety of colorful yarn
* scissors

To Do:
1) Cut slits along the top and bottom edges of the cardboard, about 1/4 inch apart. (Make sure the top and bottom of the cardboard are the same length.) Use a ruler and pencil to help you measure even segments. The closer the slits are to each other, the tighter the weave will be.

2) To make a loom, wrap the twine lengthwise between the slits on the cardboard. Start at one corner of the cardboard and thread the twine up and around each slit. When you reach the end of the cardboard, cut the twine and fasten in place.

3) Students can now weave yarn over and under the twine. They can either use one color of yarn or experiment with using different colors to create designs. As students weave, make sure they push the rows of yarn together and leave no space in between.

4) When the cardboard is covered with their weaving, tie off the ends of the yarn and the twine and remove the cardboard.

ATALANTA AND THE GREAT RACE

Atalanta was tricked into losing the race by some golden apples. Apples are the fruit part of the apple tree, the part we eat. We eat many other fruits, but we also eat other parts of plants as well. Conduct a plant guessing game with your class. The object is to come up with as many foods as possible that are certain parts of a plant. On the board or on chart paper, make a chart with six columns. Label the columns "Roots," "Seeds," "Fruits," "Flowers," "Leaves," and "Stems." Invite students to come up with as many edible plants as they can for each column. Here are some examples of each:

ROOTS	SEEDS	FRUITS	FLOWERS	LEAVES	STEMS
carrots	lima beans	tomatoes	broccoli	kale	celery
beets	peas	apples	cauliflower	lettuce	rhubarb
turnips	green beans	cucumbers	squash blossoms	spinach	asparagus
rutabagas	sunflower seeds	strawberries	nasturtiums	cabbage	
	black-eyed peas	blueberries		collards	
	pinto beans			mustard	

DAEDALUS AND ICARUS

Daedalus created wings that helped both him and Icarus fly out of the tower. Invite your class to be as inventive as Daedalus and create their own version of Daedalus's wings—paper airplanes. Have them experiment with different styles and materials. Size, shape, and type of paper are just some of the variables that could be altered. Then have students take their planes on some test runs. Students can make a chart listing each plane, then measure and record the length and/or duration of each one's flight. What, if anything, can students deduce from this experiment? Did one type of paper work better than another? Did smaller planes fly better than larger ones or vice versa?

KING MIDAS AND THE GOLDEN TOUCH

Midas was given one wish, and he wished for gold. Invite students to write about what they would most wish for, given the opportunity. Have them explain why they desire that particular thing, and then have them think about what the consequences might be if their wish were granted. As they have learned from the story, sometimes you have to be careful what you wish for.

THE TROJAN HORSE

Your class may not be able to build a giant Trojan Horse, but they can build other sculptures—from toothpicks and gumdrops or marshmallows! This activity is creative fun for kids of all ages, and the possibilities are endless. Simply provide students with lots of toothpicks and gumdrops or marshmallows and let their imaginations run wild. Students may want to attempt to make a horse sculpture, but any three-dimensional structure is fine. You may want to use slightly stale gumdrops or marshmallows because they get firmer as they get older and are better at holding up a sculpture. This may also discourage students from eating the materials!

THE GODS AND GODDESSES BAKE-OFF

CHARACTERS

CHORUS 1
CHORUS 2
ZEUS (ZOOS)
HERA (HEER-uh)
POSEIDON (poh-SY-duhn)
HADES (HAY-deez)
DEMETER (di-MEE-tuhr)
HESTIA (HES-tee-uh)
HEBE (HEE-bee)

APOLLO (uh-PAH-loh)
ARTEMIS (AR-tuh-mis)
ATHENA (uh-THEE-nuh)
HEPHAESTUS (heh-FEHS-tus)
APHRODITE (af-reh-DY-tee)
HERMES (HER-meez)
ARES (AIR-eez)
DIONYSUS (dy-uh-NY-sus)

CHORUS 1: High above the clouds on Mount Olympus, the highest mountain in Greece, lived the gods and goddesses who controlled all that happened on Earth.

CHORUS 2: Leader of them all was Zeus, king of the gods and goddesses. He sat upon his throne with his wife, Hera, at his side.

17

Greek Myth Plays © 2008 by Carol Pugliano-Martin, Scholastic Teaching Resources

CHORUS 1:	They were dining on ambrosia, the food of the gods.
CHORUS 2:	And washing it down with nectar, the drink of the gods.
ZEUS:	You know, Hera, I've been thinking.
HERA:	What is it, dear?
ZEUS:	I'm tired of eating ambrosia and drinking nectar.
HERA:	Mmm-hmm.
ZEUS:	I'm serious. Day in and day out, it's always the same thing. Ambrosia and nectar, ambrosia and nectar. It's time for a change.
HERA:	What do you suggest, dear?
ZEUS:	A gods and goddesses bake-off!
HERA:	Um, that's fine, dear, but there's one problem.
ZEUS:	What's that?
HERA:	They can change the seasons, calm the seas, and send people to the underworld, but there's one thing the gods and goddesses can't do. They can't bake.
ZEUS:	Well, they've never had much of a chance, have they? Let's give it a try.
CHORUS 1:	So Zeus summoned all of the gods and goddesses to his palace.
CHORUS 2:	He instructed them all to bring a cake that they baked themselves.
ZEUS:	Welcome, all! I hope you all had fun baking. I'm looking forward to sampling your creations. I, too, have baked, and I know you will enjoy my contribution. Let's start with mine, of course. Wheel it out, servants!
HERA:	Um, honey. It's gigantic.
ZEUS:	Well, of course. What else would you expect from the king of the gods!
HERA:	Well, let's have some.

Greek Myth Plays © 2008 by Carol Pugliano-Martin, Scholastic Teaching Resources

ZEUS:	Have some? Oh, no! You must not cut it. It will be ruined!
HERA:	Well, we've got to eat something, but since I am the goddess of marriage, I will not fight with you.
ZEUS:	Poseidon, what have you brought?
POSEIDON:	Here is my creation, brother.
ZEUS:	Hmm, looks good. Now for a taste. (*He cuts a piece and takes a bite.*) Acch! It's too watery!
POSEIDON:	Of course it's watery! I'm the god of the sea!
ZEUS:	Next, my brother Hades. What have you brought?
HADES:	Here! Great, huh?
ZEUS:	Well, it's black. Interesting for a cake. Let me taste. (*He takes a bite.*) Blech! This is burnt!
HADES:	What do you expect from the god of the underworld?
ZEUS:	Quick, Hebe, my daughter. You are the cupbearer to the gods. Bring me a drink! Nectar!
HEBE:	You have banned nectar, Father. Here is some lemonade.
ZEUS:	Lemonade. Interesting. Sweet. Tart. Delicious. Now if only I had some good cake. Let's try another.
DEMETER:	Sample mine, brother. It's full of healthy grains and ripe fruits.
ZEUS:	Yuck! It's too, too . . . good for me. I don't like my cakes to be so healthy, even though you are the goddess of the harvest.
HESTIA:	(*Comforting Demeter*) Come, sister. I have a nice fire going in the fireplace. You can relax there.
DEMETER:	I can always count on you, Hestia. You truly are the goddess of the hearth and home.
ZEUS:	Apollo, my son! This party needs to be livened up. Show us why you are the god of music. Play us a tune!

Greek Myth Plays © 2008 by Carol Pugliano-Martin, Scholastic Teaching Resources

APOLLO: Of course, Father. How about this jaunty number I wrote myself? (*Pretends to play a lyre*)

ZEUS: (*Sounding pleased*) Lovely! Artemis, my daughter, have you brought a cake?

ARTEMIS: Come on, Dad, me? Bake? I'm the goddess of hunting, remember?

ZEUS: Yes, yes. I don't know why you won't find a nice young god and settle down.

ARTEMIS: Well, that wouldn't seem right since I'm also the goddess of unmarried girls.

ZEUS: Never mind. Where's my favorite daughter? Where's Athena?

ATHENA: Here I am, Father.

ZEUS: And what have you baked for me?

ATHENA: Well, I didn't bake. I figured there would be many cakes and not enough pottery plates, so I made these dishes for the occasion.

ZEUS: My dear. No wonder you are both the goddess of wisdom and arts and crafts. You are smart as well as talented.

ARES: (*Annoyed*) Oh, please. You said bake, not make pottery!

ZEUS: Ares, my son, why must you always start a fight?

ARES: I am the god of war. What do you expect?

APHRODITE: Why must we fight? Love is all we need.

HEPHAESTUS: (*Lovingly, to Aphrodite*) Ah, that's why I married you, Aphrodite, you goddess of love, you. Here is my cake, Father.

ZEUS: Um . . . son . . . Hephaestus . . . it's on fire.

HEPHAESTUS: Of course. I'm the god of fire. I must express myself in the only way I know how.

APHRODITE: I think it's beautiful!

Greek Myth Plays © 2008 by Carol Pugliano-Martin, Scholastic Teaching Resources

HEPHAESTUS: Thanks, babe.

HERMES: (*Sounding out of breath*) Hi, Pop. Sorry I'm late. I just flew in. Lots of messages to deliver for you, you know? Gotta go now and watch over the shepherds, merchants, travelers, and, yes, even thieves. Why on earth am I the god of so many things?

ZEUS: Hello and good-bye, Hermes. Okay, let's see. That leaves only Dionysus. Please tell me you brought a cake, my son. I'm very hungry.

DIONYSUS: Here it is, Father.

ZEUS: Looks good. But let's give it a taste. (*Hiccups*) This cake is filled with wine!

DIONYSUS: Sorry. It's one of the only ingredients I had. As the god of wine, I've got bottles of it coming out my ears.

ZEUS: (*Wearily*) Yes, I know. Well, after this bake-off of the gods and goddesses, I guess there's only one thing left to say.

HERA: What's that, dear?

ZEUS: Pass the ambrosia!

THE END

Greek Myth Plays © 2008 by Carol Pugliano-Martin, Scholastic Teaching Resources

Glossary

highness: a title of honor for royalty

ambrosia: the food of the gods

nectar: the drink of the gods

summoned: called or requested someone to come

sampling: trying a small amount of something to see if you like it

cupbearer: Hestia is the cupbearer to the gods, which means she serves the other gods and goddesses their drinks.

banned: forbidden

tart: tasting sour or sharp

hearth: the area in front of a fireplace

lyre: a small, stringed, harplike instrument played mostly in ancient Egypt, Israel, and Greece

jaunty: giving a carefree and self-confident impression

number: word sometimes used by musicians to mean "song"

merchants: people who sell goods for profit

Greek Myth Plays © 2008 by Carol Pugliano-Martin, Scholastic Teaching Resources

PANDORA'S BOX

CHARACTERS

CHORUS 1
CHORUS 2
ZEUS (ZOOS)
PROMETHEUS
  (pro-MEE-thee-us)
EPIMETHEUS
  (ep-uh-MEE-thee-us)
APHRODITE
  (af-reh-DY-tee)
HERMES (HER-meez)
APOLLO (uh-PAH-loh)
PANDORA (pan-DOR-ah)

DISEASE
CRUELTY
PAIN
OLD AGE
DISAPPOINTMENT
HATE
JEALOUSY
WAR
DEATH
HOPE

Greek Myth Plays © 2008 by Carol Pugliano-Martin, Scholastic Teaching Resources

CHORUS 1: Zeus, king of the gods, was angry with Prometheus for giving the gift of fire to the mortals.

CHORUS 2: He was also angry with the mortals for taking the gift. He would punish Prometheus and the mortals.

CHORUS 1: Epimetheus, Prometheus's brother, would help him punish the mortals, although Epimetheus didn't know it.

CHORUS 2: One day, Zeus called the brothers to him.

ZEUS:	Come here, my friends.
EPIMETHEUS:	Here we are.
PROMETHEUS:	What is it, Zeus?
ZEUS:	Well, first of all, Prometheus. You gave the gift of fire to the mortals. I am very angry about that. Such a wonderful thing should be only for gods like us, not lowly mortals.
PROMETHEUS:	Sorry, Zeus.
ZEUS:	You will be severely punished for what you've done. I'll deal with you later. Now Epimetheus.
EPIMETHEUS:	Y-y-yes, Zeus.
ZEUS:	To you, I have a gift. A wife! I made her myself with some help from the other gods.
EPIMETHEUS:	Great! What is she like?
ZEUS:	See for yourself. Gods, bring in Pandora!
APHRODITE:	Here she is. I have given her beauty so she can please your eyes.
HERMES:	I have given her a clever tongue so she can amuse you.
APOLLO:	I have given her the gift of music so she can entertain you.
CHORUS 1:	Zeus had given her the gift of curiosity.
CHORUS 2:	But he didn't mention that to Epimetheus.
EPIMETHEUS:	Wow, she's wonderful. Thank you, Zeus.
PROMETHEUS:	No fair!
ZEUS:	(*To Prometheus*) Never mind, you. (*To Epimetheus and Pandora*) Go and live happily together. Oh, yes, take this box as a wedding gift. (*Zeus hands Epimetheus a box.*) But you must never, ever open it.
EPIMETHEUS:	We won't. It's beautiful. Thank you again.

Greek Myth Plays © 2008 by Carol Pugliano-Martin, Scholastic Teaching Resources

CHORUS 1:	So Zeus punished Prometheus by chaining him to a rock, while Epimetheus went home with his new wife.
CHORUS 2:	Little did they know, Zeus's plan to punish the mortals was about to unfold.
PANDORA:	Okay, Epi, we're in our own home now. Let's see what's in the box.
EPIMETHEUS:	Oh, no, Pandora. I promised Zeus we wouldn't.
PANDORA:	You are a married god now. You don't have to listen to Zeus.
EPIMETHEUS:	Yes, I do, and you should too. He is a very powerful god—the most powerful. If he says don't open the box, you don't open the box, and that's that. (*He leaves.*)
PANDORA:	Hmm . . . *I* didn't promise anything. But maybe Epimetheus is right. Still, what could happen? It seems like a harmless box. There are probably some fine dishes or jewels in it. I must find out! No, I shouldn't. But it's *my* wedding present too. I will!
CHORUS 1:	Don't do it, Pandora!
CHORUS 2:	Listen to your husband and to almighty Zeus.
PANDORA:	I don't have to listen to anyone! Go away!
CHORUS 1 & 2:	You'll be sorry!
CHORUS 1:	Pandora took a little gold key and opened the box a crack.
PANDORA:	(*Opening the box*) Just a little peek . . .
CHORUS 2:	Suddenly, out popped the world's Miseries, ready to wreak havoc on the unsuspecting mortals!
DISEASE:	Ah-hah! You foolish girl! You have let us out!
PANDORA:	Who are you?
DISEASE:	I am Disease. Now man shall get sick.
CRUELTY:	I am Cruelty. Now men shall be mean to one another.

Greek Myth Plays © 2008 by Carol Pugliano-Martin, Scholastic Teaching Resources

PAIN: I am Pain. Man shall now hurt.

OLD AGE: I am Old Age. Pretty self-explanatory.

DISAPPOINTMENT: I'm Disappointment. Now man shall feel let down.

HATE: I'm Hate. Man will now dislike others.

JEALOUSY: I am Jealousy. Man will now yearn for the things others have.

WAR: I'm War. Man will not live in peace.

DEATH: And I am Death. Man will not live forever!

PANDORA: What have I done?

HOPE: (*Sweetly, peeking out from the box*) You have played out Zeus's punishment to man for accepting Prometheus's gift of fire. These Miseries will go out among man and cause them much suffering.

PANDORA: Well, who are *you*? You don't seem very miserable.

HOPE: I am Hope. Keep me in the box. The Miseries will go out among the mortals. But I will remain so that humans will always have me in spite of all the evils that have gone out among them. I will help them bear the pain, but only if I remain safe inside this box.

PANDORA: Oh. Okay. Bye-bye now.

CHORUS 1: And so Pandora shut the box, leaving Hope inside to help man bear the new Miseries.

CHORUS 2: And to this day, when someone "opens Pandora's box," he or she causes trouble.

PANDORA: Some wedding gift! I really wanted a toaster!

THE END

Greek Myth Plays © 2008 by Carol Pugliano-Martin, Scholastic Teaching Resources

Glossary

mortals: human beings

lowly: having a low rank or position

severely: very harshly

curiosity: eagerness to find things out

unfold: to become known

harmless: not able to cause injury or damage

almighty: possessing total power

miseries: things that cause great discomfort or unhappiness

wreak: to cause

havoc: great damage and chaos

unsuspecting: the state of not knowing something will happen

self-explanatory: not needing any further explanation

in spite of: without being hindered by, or in defiance of

Greek Myth Plays © 2008 by Carol Pugliano-Martin. Scholastic Teaching Resources

ECHO AND NARCISSUS

CHARACTERS

Chorus 1
Chorus 2
Zeus (ZOOS)
Hera (HEER-uh)
Nymph 1 (NIMF)
Nymph 2
Echo (ECK-oh)
Narcissus (nar-SIS-us)

Greek Myth Plays © 2008 by Carol Pugliano-Martin, Scholastic Teaching Resources

CHORUS 1:   Zeus, the mightiest of the gods, was married to Hera, the goddess of marriage.

CHORUS 2:   Zeus, being a powerful god, was popular with the ladies. He liked to flirt. As you will see, Hera will have none of it.

ZEUS: Ah, what a beautiful day! I think I'll pop on down to Earth and walk in the woods a bit.

HERA: A walk in the woods, huh? Are you sure you're not going down there to flirt with the nymphs?

ZEUS: Flirt? Nymphs? Me? Don't be silly. Why would I flirt with nymphs when I have a beautiful wife like you?

HERA: Well, perhaps you're right. Okay, go for your walk. Be home for dinner.

ZEUS: Ta-ta, my dear!

CHORUS 1: Hera, what is this?

CHORUS 2: Are you really going to believe Zeus's story?

HERA: No way. He must be kidding. I trust him about as far as I can throw him, and that isn't far. Oh, well. It's nothing that a little careful spying won't take care of.

CHORUS 1: Now that sounds more like our Hera!

CHORUS 2: Meanwhile, on Earth, three nymphs are in a meadow.

NYMPH 1: What a beautiful day for picking flowers!

NYMPH 2: It's awesome!

ECHO: (*Speaking very quickly*) Well, the weather report showed a cold front moving in. Soon there will be clouds and pretty heavy winds. Maybe even some rain. I really don't mind the rain, though. It does help these beautiful flowers grow. And I love flowers. I think my favorite is the violet. However, I'm also quite fond of the evening primrose.

NYMPH 1: Echo, slow down.

NYMPH 2: You sure love to talk!

ZEUS: Ladies, ladies, good morning! How are you?

NYMPH 1: (*Giggling*) Oh, hello, Zeus.

NYMPH 2: (*In a flirty tone of voice*) It's so nice to see you.

ECHO: Look, here comes Hera.

Greek Myth Plays © 2008 by Carol Pugliano-Martin, Scholastic Teaching Resources

ZEUS: Oh, no! My wife! Echo, be a dear. Distract Hera while my friends here and I make a quick get away. Thanks, love!

CHORUS 1: Echo has a job to do.

CHORUS 2: She must distract Hera with her gift of gab.

CHORUS 1: Will Hera fall for it?

CHORUS 2: (*To Chorus 1*) Come now. You know her better than that!

HERA: I was sure I heard Zeus's voice. And some high-pitched giggling. That can only mean one thing. Now where are they?

ECHO: Good morning, Hera.

HERA: Oh, hello, Echo. Have you seen my husband?

ECHO: Seen? Hmm . . . Well, I'm not sure I would trust my eyes right now. You see, this early spring pollen really makes my eyes water and I can't see very well with my eyes all teared-up. I never used to suffer from allergies, but now it's sneeze, sneeze, sneeze, all the time.

HERA: Hush, girl. I'm sure I heard him, and I think you know where he is. Now tell me!

ECHO: Well, you know sounds can be deceiving. Once I thought I heard a Cyclops coming toward me. I was sure of it. I panicked and hid, shaking all the while. Turned out it was just a gentle deer walking among the leaves. And there I was shaking in my sandals. By the way, those are lovely sandals you're wearing. Where did you get them?

HERA: Enough! I'm sure he got away by now, thanks to your chatter. From now on you will be almost silent. You will only be able to speak the last words someone else says!

ECHO: Else says. (*Gasps as Hera storms off*)

CHORUS 1: Sorry, Echo.

CHORUS 2: We thought you knew better.

CHORUS 1: Enter Narcissus.

Greek Myth Plays © 2008 by Carol Pugliano-Martin, Scholastic Teaching Resources

CHORUS 2:   A man who is his own best friend.

NARCISSUS: I love me.
It's me I love.
My beauty comes from
The gods above.

ECHO: (*From her hiding place*) Gods above.

NARCISSUS: Who's there?

ECHO: Who's there?

NARCISSUS: Come out!

ECHO: Come out!

NARCISSUS: Oh, so you're playing a joke on me! Well, I won't have it! Show yourself this instant!

ECHO: (*Coming out of hiding*) This instant.

NARCISSUS: Silly girl. I suppose you are so awestruck by my beauty that you have lost the ability to speak properly. Surely you love me.

ECHO: Love me.

NARCISSUS: Love you? Never. No one is good enough for me. How dare you love me.

ECHO: (*Holding out her arms toward Narcissus*) Love me! Love me!

NARCISSUS: Ahhh!!!!! (*Runs away*)

ECHO: (*Quietly*) Ahhh!

CHORUS 1:   And so Narcissus rejects Echo . . .

CHORUS 2:   As he has done to so many nymphs before.

NARCISSUS: Imagine that girl thinking I could love her. Hah! She's just like all the rest. Oh, well. Who can blame them? I am quite the dreamboat. And speaking of boat, here's a delightful pond. I think I'll have a drink.

Greek Myth Plays © 2008 by Carol Pugliano-Martin, Scholastic Teaching Resources

CHORUS 1: Narcissus bends down to drink from the pond. Echo sees Narcissus and hides so she can watch him.

NARCISSUS: (*Seeing his reflection in the pond*) Well, well, what do we have here? Hello, my lovely. (*He pauses.*) Oh, you're shy. How charming. You certainly are beautiful. (*He pauses again.*) Oh, well, no need to speak. I'm happy just to lie here and gaze upon you. Hmm . . . perhaps just one small kiss as well . . .

CHORUS 2: Silly Narcissus bends toward the water to kiss his reflection. But as soon as he touches the water his reflection disappears.

NARCISSUS: Oh, no! Where did you go? Oh, I have frightened you away. Please come back! (*He waits.*) Oh, thank goodness, there you are. I'll behave and just look at you.

CHORUS 1: Narcissus gazes lovingly at his reflection.

NARCISSUS: I can't stand it. I must embrace you!

CHORUS 2: Narcissus grabs at the water, and his reflection disappears altogether.

NARCISSUS: You're gone! Oh, I can't live without you! I won't! Good-bye, cruel world!

ECHO: (*Noticeably upset*) Cruel world.

CHORUS 1: (*to Narcissus*) Narcissus? Narcissus? (*To audience*) He has died of love for himself!

CHORUS 2: Look! Where he lay there is now a flower. It shall be called a narcissus.

CHORUS 1: And what became of Echo? She fled to a cave and also perished from love for Narcissus.

CHORUS 2: If you are ever near that cave, you will hear her speak the last words anyone says.

CHORUS 1: Look, here come Zeus and the nymphs!

NYMPH 1: (*Looking at the narcissus flower*) Hey, cool flower!

NYMPH 2: It's awesome! Can I have it, Zeusy?

Greek Myth Plays © 2008 by Carol Pugliano-Martin, Scholastic Teaching Resources

ZEUS:	Of course, my pet.
CHORUS 2:	Watch it, Zeus! Here comes Hera!
HERA:	(*Angrily*) Ah-hah!
ZEUS:	(*Panicked*) Hera! So . . . so . . . nice to . . . Lovely day . . . um . . . Let's get out of here! (*Runs off with the Nymphs*)
HERA:	(*To audience, as she goes after Zeus and the Nymphs*) Gods!
CHORUS 1:	Let's go!
CHORUS 2:	Yeah, we don't want to miss this!

THE END

Glossary

popular: liked or enjoyed by many people

flirt: to play at being in love with someone

nymphs: in ancient Greek and Roman stories, beautiful female spirits or goddesses who lived in a forest, meadow, or stream

cold front: a movement of cold air which causes a change in the weather

distract: to weaken someone's concentration on what they are doing

gab: to chat or to gossip

pollen: tiny yellow grains produced in flowers. Some people are allergic to pollen.

deceiving: having the ability to trick you into believing something that is not true

panicked: suddenly felt great terror or fright

awestruck: suddenly hit with a feeling of admiration and respect, possibly mixed with a little fear

perished: died or was destroyed

Greek Myth Plays © 2008 by Carol Pugliano-Martin, Scholastic Teaching Resources

DEMETER AND PERSEPHONE

CHARACTERS

CHORUS 1
CHORUS 2
DEMETER
 (di-MEE-tuhr)
PERSEPHONE
 (per-SEF-uh-nee)
HADES (HAY-deez)
ZEUS (ZOOS)
HECATE (HECK-uh-tee)
HELIOS (HEE-lee-us)

CHORUS 1:   You know how in some places, it is cold for part of the year and warm for the other part?

CHORUS 2:   Well, there's a reason for that. Hear now the story of Demeter and Persephone.

CHORUS 1:   One day, Demeter, the goddess of the harvest, was in the fields with her daughter, Persephone.

CHORUS 2:   Persephone was a beautiful young girl, and Demeter worshipped the ground she walked on.

DEMETER: Come along, my darling girl. We must go home now.

Greek Myth Plays © 2008 by Carol Pugliano-Martin, Scholastic Teaching Resources

PERSEPHONE: Oh, Mother, not now. Just a few more minutes. There are so many beautiful flowers to pick.

DEMETER: My sweet, wonderful child, all right. I am going to sit under this tree for a while. Go and find some flowers that are as beautiful as you are, if that's possible.

PERSEPHONE: Oh, Mom. Give it a rest.

DEMETER: Such a sweet girl.

CHORUS 1: Meanwhile, down in the Underworld, Hades, the god of that dark place, was unhappy.

CHORUS 2: He was being visited by his brother Zeus, the king of the gods.

HADES: It's so dark down here. Dark, dreary, dull. The only thing that might brighten it up a bit is a beautiful queen.

ZEUS: Yes, my brother. But, no offense, what woman would marry you?

HADES: Hey, listen. I have my own place, my own chariot, and I'm a king. What more could any woman want?

ZEUS: Hmm. You have a point. Well, do you have anyone in mind?

HADES: As a matter of fact, I do. Lovely Persephone.

ZEUS: Demeter's beloved daughter? There's no way. I cannot allow it. Besides, Demeter would never let her go.

HADES: I know. That is why I have a plan.

CHORUS 1: So Hades told Zeus his plan to steal Persephone.

CHORUS 2: Zeus, being a loyal brother, did nothing to stand in the way of Hades' plot.

CHORUS 1: Back on Earth, Persephone found a flower that Hades had placed in the field.

PERSEPHONE: Ooooh! Look at that narcissus! I've never seen one that was this dark red color. I must have it.

Greek Myth Plays © 2008 by Carol Pugliano-Martin, Scholastic Teaching Resources

CHORUS 2: As Persephone bent to pick the flower, Hades arrived in his chariot and swept Persephone away.

PERSEPHONE: Whoa!

HADES: You're mine! All mine!!

PERSEPHONE: Help me! Mother!

CHORUS 1: But Demeter had fallen asleep under the tree and could not hear the cries of her daughter. Soon, she woke up.

DEMETER: Persephone? Where are you, my precious child? Oh, these young girls, they are such rebels. Persephone? Darling girl?

CHORUS 2: Demeter ran into Hecate, the moon god, who was snoozing in the field.

DEMETER: Hecate, have you seen Persephone?

HECATE: I have not. It is day, and I was asleep.

DEMETER: Oh, what good are you? I must find my daughter!

HECATE: Why don't you ask Helios, the sun god. He sees everything in the day.

DEMETER: Good idea. I take back what I said earlier.

HECATE: No problem.

CHORUS 1: Demeter went to see Helios.

HELIOS: Yes, I have seen Persephone. But you will not like what I have to say.

DEMETER: Say it, Sunny. I must have my daughter back!

HELIOS: Hades has taken her to the Underworld to be his queen.

DEMETER: What? How could this happen? Who would allow it?

HELIOS: You might want to check in with Zeus. That's all I'll say.

Greek Myth Plays © 2008 by Carol Pugliano-Martin, Scholastic Teaching Resources

CHORUS 2:	Meanwhile, back in the Underworld, Hades was happy, but Persephone was miserable.
HADES:	Ah, you sure have brightened up the place with your beauty.
PERSEPHONE:	Get me out of here!
HADES:	Sure, it's dark. There are the souls of the dead roaming around. But you'll get used to it.
PERSEPHONE:	Never! I must get back to my mother.
HADES:	How about a little snack? You must be hungry.
PERSEPHONE:	Save it, buddy. I won't eat your food.
CHORUS 1:	Demeter went to see Zeus. He admitted that he did not stand in the way of Hades' plan to abduct Persephone.
DEMETER:	You what?
ZEUS:	Well, he's not so bad, is he? He's a powerful man, successful.
DEMETER:	How could you allow it?
ZEUS:	Look, he's my brother. He was lonely. He was sad.
DEMETER:	Well, you are going to be sad when you hear what I'm about to say. As long as my daughter is down there, nothing will grow here on Earth.
ZEUS:	Well, that won't affect me. I'm a god and don't eat mortal food.
DEMETER:	Yes, but who worships you? The mortals! If they starve, there will be no one to praise and honor you.
ZEUS:	What? No one to glorify the name of Zeus?! I can't have that! I must be glorified!
DEMETER:	I knew you'd see my point.
ZEUS:	Okay. I'll return your daughter to you. I just hope she hasn't eaten anything down there.

Greek Myth Plays © 2008 by Carol Pugliano-Martin, Scholastic Teaching Resources

DEMETER:	My girl knows better than that!
ZEUS:	We'll see.
CHORUS 2:	But Persephone did not know that whoever eats food from the Underworld may never leave.
CHORUS 1:	Hades was trying his best to get Persephone to eat.
HADES:	(*Holding out a pomegranate*) Just a tiny morsel, my dear. To keep up your strength.
PERSEPHONE:	Well, maybe just a few of these juicy pomegranate seeds. What harm could they do?
CHORUS 2:	Persephone, no!
CHORUS 1:	Don't eat them!
PERSEPHONE:	Hey, who asked you? You're as bad as my mother.
CHORUS 2:	Suit yourself.
PERSEPHONE:	I will.
CHORUS 1 & 2:	Hmph!
PERSEPHONE:	Hmph!
CHORUS 1 & 2:	Go ahead and be foolish.
PERSEPHONE:	I know you are, but what am I?
HADES:	Oh, will you all stop it?! Here, my dear.
PERSEPHONE:	(*Eating some seeds*) Juicy!
HADES:	Ah-hah! Now you can never leave me. You have eaten food from the Underworld!
PERSEPHONE:	That was a dirty trick!
CHORUS 1:	Just then, Demeter and Zeus arrive.

Greek Myth Plays © 2008 by Carol Pugliano-Martin, Scholastic Teaching Resources

DEMETER:	My baby!
PERSEPHONE:	Mother!
ZEUS:	Hand her over, Hades.
HADES:	Wait a minute. You said it was okay.
ZEUS:	Well, I changed my mind. The king of the gods can do that, you know.
HADES:	Well, you are too late. Persephone has eaten.
DEMETER:	Persephone, how could you?
PERSEPHONE:	Oh, Mother, lay off. I was so hungry and I just had six tiny, little pomegranate seeds.
DEMETER:	Of course, my precious. Why am I criticizing the most wonderful thing in my life? Oh, Zeus, is there nothing you can do?
ZEUS:	Six tiny seeds hardly seems to warrant staying down here for eternity. How about this? Since Persephone ate only six seeds, she will stay down here for six months of the year. The other six can be spent above with Demeter.
HADES:	Well, I guess six months is better than none at all.
DEMETER:	True. But for the six months that my daughter is away, nothing shall grow on Earth.
ZEUS:	Demeter!
DEMETER:	Let me finish. I will show the mortals how to harvest food and save it for the months Persephone is here. I think I deserve a break as well. I will rest during that time. Then I will rejoice with a bountiful growing season for the return of my beloved Persephone.
PERSEPHONE:	Do I have any say in this?
HADES, ZEUS, AND DEMETER:	NO!
PERSEPHONE:	Just asking.

Greek Myth Plays © 2008 by Carol Pugliano-Martin, Scholastic Teaching Resources

CHORUS 2:	And so it was then, and so it is now.
DEMETER:	And remember, Mommy loves you!
PERSEPHONE:	Can it, Mother!
DEMETER:	Yes, my sweet.

THE END

Glossary

dreary: dull and miserable

offense: If you cause offense, you upset someone.

chariot: a small vehicle pulled by a horse or horses, used in ancient times for battle or for racing

narcissus: a plant that grows from a bulb and has yellow or white flowers and long, thin leaves

precious: very special or dear

rebels: people who fight against the people in charge of something

abduct: to kidnap someone

morsel: a small piece of food

pomegranate: a round, reddish yellow fruit that has a tough skin, red flesh, and many seeds

criticizing: telling someone what he or she has done wrong

warrant: to deserve

eternity: time without beginning or end; a seemingly endless time period

Greek Myth Plays © 2008 by Carol Pugliano-Martin, Scholastic Teaching Resources

ORPHEUS AND EURYDICE

CHARACTERS

CHORUS 1
CHORUS 2
ORPHEUS (OR-fee-us)
APOLLO (uh-PAH-loh)
EURYDICE
　(yu-RID-uh-see)
ARISTAEUS
　(ar-ee-STEE-us)

CHARON (KAR-on)
CERBERUS 1
　(SER-ber-us)
CERBERUS 2
CERBERUS 3
HADES (HAY-deez)
PERSEPHONE
　(per-SEF-uh-nee)

CHORUS 1: It is said that to trust is one of the most difficult things a mortal can do.

CHORUS 2: And few people know that more than Orpheus, whose lack of trust cost him love.

ORPHEUS: Father, I have fallen in love! I wish to be married! She's the most wonderful woman, well, nymph, in the world. Her name is Eurydice.

APOLLO: Eurydice. Ah yes, I know of her. She certainly is lovely. I give you my permission to marry her.

CHORUS 1: And so Orpheus and Eurydice were married.

CHORUS 2: Never before was there a happier couple.

EURYDICE: Orpheus, please play for me on your lyre. I've never heard such beautiful music.

ORPHEUS: And I've never felt more like playing. Being with you makes my music sound better.

Greek Myth Plays © 2008 by Carol Pugliano-Martin, Scholastic Teaching Resources

CHORUS 1:   Orpheus was the finest musician around.

CHORUS 2:   His music charmed savage beasts and made all those around him feel happy and peaceful.

EURYDICE: My love, while you are playing, I think I will pick some flowers up on that hill. Your music will follow me and keep me company as I gather some blossoms.

ORPHEUS: I will play, my sweet. And I will eagerly await your return.

CHORUS 1:   So, Eurydice went to pick flowers. As she strolled through the field, she was comforted by the sounds of Orpheus's lyre.

CHORUS 2:   But Aristaeus, a hunter, spied Eurydice walking and pursued her.

ARISTAEUS: Why pick flowers when you are more lovely than any flower could ever be?

EURYDICE: Leave me alone, Aristaeus. I am wed to Orpheus and belong only to him.

ARISTAEUS: That puny musician! I am a hunter. I can provide for you. Meat sustains a person more than music.

EURYDICE: I said, leave me alone!

ARISTAEUS: I will not!

CHORUS 1:   And with that, Aristaeus began chasing Eurydice through the woods. He was a hunter and was very swift, but eventually Eurydice was able to get away from him.

ARISTAEUS: Drats!

CHORUS 2:   But alas, Eurydice was so panicked that she was not watching where she was going. She stepped on a viper whose bite filled her with poison, and she died. The last sound she heard was Orpheus's lyre singing through the trees as she traveled down to the Underworld.

ORPHEUS: Where is my Eurydice? She's been gone such a long time.

CHORUS 1:   She's gone to the Underworld, Orpheus.

Greek Myth Plays © 2008 by Carol Pugliano-Martin, Scholastic Teaching Resources

CHORUS 2: A viper has taken her from you.

ORPHEUS: No, not my beloved Eurydice! I won't allow it! I must get her back. Father!

APOLLO: I'm afraid there's nothing that can be done, my son. The dead cannot return to the land of the living. I'm sorry.

ORPHEUS: I will not accept it. I am going to her!

APOLLO: Orpheus, no!

CHORUS 1: But it was too late. Nothing would keep Orpheus from his Eurydice.

CHORUS 2: With lyre in hand, he traveled down to the Underworld and reached the River Styx, which separated the land of the living from the land of the dead. There he met Charon, ferryman to the dead.

ORPHEUS: Charon, row me across. I must get my Eurydice back!

CHARON: You must be kidding. You know I transport only the dead to the other side. In fact, wasn't that your wife I just rowed across?

ORPHEUS: You've seen my Eurydice! Take me to her, Charon. I must see her!

CHARON: Sorry, pal. Until you take your last breath, you won't be riding in my boat.

CHORUS 1: Orpheus was desperate. He had to get to Eurydice. Suddenly he had an idea.

CHORUS 2: He took out his lyre and began to play the most beautiful music Charon had ever heard. It moved him to tears with its loveliness.

CHARON: (*Visibly moved*) Oh, all right. Come aboard. I'll take you across.

CHORUS 1: So Charon rowed Orpheus across the River Styx to the land of the dead.

CHORUS 2: When they reached the other side, they were greeted by Cerberus, the three-headed dog.

CERBERUS 1: Go . . .

Greek Myth Plays © 2008 by Carol Pugliano-Martin, Scholastic Teaching Resources

CERBERUS 2:   a- . . .

CERBERUS 3:   way!

CHARON: It's Cerberus, Hades' three-headed dog. I rowed you across, but he'll never let you in. He's fierce, I tell you!

CERBERUS 1:   Leave . . .

CERBERUS 2:   this . . .

CERBERUS 3:   place!

CHORUS 1:   Again, Orpheus took up his lyre and began to play. Before long, the dog was laying at Orpheus's feet getting a belly rub.

ORPHEUS: There now, good boy, uh, boys. Anyway, see ya!

HADES: I smell a living man here in the Underworld! Who dares to enter?

ORPHEUS: It is I, Orpheus, and I've come to take Eurydice home with me.

HADES: Home? Hah! She *is* home. This is now her home, Orpheus.

ORPHEUS: No, she was taken too soon. I must have her back. She'll come to you eventually, but not now!

CHORUS 2:   Persephone knew what Orpheus was going through. She had to live half the year in the Underworld. For the other half, she could stay in the land of the living with her mother, Demeter.

CHORUS 1:   Persephone, can't you help on Orpheus's behalf?

PERSEPHONE: Hades, maybe you can reconsider. I know how painful it is to be taken from those you love. I miss my mother terribly when I am down here for half the year.

HADES: I won't. She died, and she's here now. And that's that.

CHORUS 2:   Once again, Orpheus used the only weapon he'd ever had. He played a tune on his lyre that was the most beautiful ever imagined. It even reduced Hades, the god of the Underworld, to tears.

CHORUS 1:   And that's no easy task!

Greek Myth Plays © 2008 by Carol Pugliano-Martin, Scholastic Teaching Resources

HADES: (*Sniffling*) Please, stop. I can't take anymore. It's too, too beautiful. Okay, Orpheus. Since you moved me to tears, and no one has ever done that, you may have your Eurydice back.

PERSEPHONE: Bravo, Orpheus.

ORPHEUS: Oh, thank you, Hades!

HADES: On one condition. I may be a softy, but I'm still king of the dead. Eurydice will follow you back to the land of the living. But you must not turn back to look at her until you are both on the other side. If you do, she will be mine forever. Deal?

ORPHEUS: Sounds simple enough. Okay, bring her to me.

CHORUS 2: Eurydice was brought to Orpheus. The two could not contain their joy at seeing each other.

EURYDICE: Orpheus!

ORPHEUS: Eurydice!

HADES: Oh, please! Now go! And remember, do not look back!

CHORUS 1: So Orpheus and Eurydice began the long journey back to the land of the living, with Eurydice walking behind Orpheus.

CHORUS 2: They made it past Cerberus, who was drooling in his sleep, still wearing three big smiles from Orpheus's playing. They met Charon at the River Styx.

ORPHEUS: Charon, row us back to the other side. Oh, Eurydice. We will be so happy again together. You have no idea how much I missed you!

CHORUS 1: Eurydice did not answer as Charon docked the boat on the other side of the River Styx.

ORPHEUS: Here we are, my love. Now let's begin the long climb upward. Soon we will be together forever away from this dark and dreary place.

CHORUS 2: Still no response from Eurydice.

ORPHEUS: Eurydice? Are you there? Of course you are, why wouldn't you be? Still, I wish you'd answer me. Well, it won't be long now.

Greek Myth Plays © 2008 by Carol Pugliano-Martin, Scholastic Teaching Resources

CHORUS 1:   The two climbed and climbed.

ORPHEUS: I see light up ahead. It won't be long now! Isn't it wonderful, Eurydice?

CHORUS 2:   Silence was the only answer Orpheus received.

ORPHEUS: This is getting frustrating! Perhaps Hades has played a trick on me and you are not there at all. But no, Persephone would not let that happen. But, what I wouldn't give to hear your sweet voice to assure me. We're far enough away from Hades. He can't see us. Surely just one little peek won't hurt. Just to be sure. Are you there, my love?

CHORUS 1:   Orpheus looked back at Eurydice.

EURYDICE: Farewell, Orpheus. (*Holding out her hands to Orpheus as she fades off*)

CHORUS 2:   And with that, Eurydice traveled back down to the Underworld, this time, forever.

ORPHEUS: Eurydice! No!

CHORUS 1:   But it was too late. Eurydice was gone.

CHORUS 2:   Orpheus returned to the land of the living. But his was no life. He was so miserable, he never played his lyre.

CHORUS 1:   Orpheus's grief eventually caused him to die. However, this was not such a bad thing for Orpheus.

CHORUS 2:   He returned to the Underworld, this time legitimately, and he and Eurydice were together forevermore.

EURYDICE: (*Adoringly*) Play it again, Orphie.

ORPHEUS: Sure thing, babe.

THE END

Greek Myth Plays © 2008 by Carol Pugliano-Martin, Scholastic Teaching Resources

Glossary

mortal: a human being

nymph: in ancient Greek and Roman stories, a beautiful female spirit or goddess who lived in a forest, meadow, or stream

lyre: a small, stringed, harplike instrument played mostly in ancient Egypt, Israel, and Greece

savage: not tamed, or not under human control

pursued: followed or chased someone in order to catch him or her

sustains: gives energy and strength to keep going

swift: moving or able to move very fast

drats: an exclamation or interjection meaning the same thing as "Darn"

panicked: suddenly felt great terror or fright

alas: unfortunately, or sadly

viper: any poisonous snake

ferryman: person who rows people and things on a boat across a river or other body of water

transport: to move people and freight from one place to another

fierce: violent or dangerous

eventually: finally or at last

behalf: If you do something on behalf of someone else, you do it for that person in his or her place.

reconsider: to think again about a previous decision, especially with the idea of making a change

docked: brought a boat alongside a wharf or port so passengers can get off

dreary: gloomy

response: answer

frustrating: having that feeling of puzzlement or confusion

assure: to promise something, or say something positively

legitimately: lawfully or rightfully

Greek Myth Plays © 2008 by Carol Pugliano-Martin, Scholastic Teaching Resources

ATHENA AND ARACHNE:
HOW SPIDERS CAME TO BE

CHARACTERS

CHORUS 1
CHORUS 2
CUSTOMER 1
CUSTOMER 2
CUSTOMER 3
ARACHNE (uh-RACK-nee)
ATHENA (uh-THEE-nuh)

CHORUS 1: Hear now the tale of Arachne.

CHORUS 2: The story of a mortal girl who challenged the gods.

CHORUS 1: Arachne was the best mortal weaver in all of Greece.

CHORUS 2: She was trained by the goddess Athena, who taught the fine arts to many people of Greece.

CUSTOMER 1: What a beautiful tapestry! I must buy it.

ARACHNE: Why, thank you very much.

CUSTOMER 2: Your work is exquisite! I, too, would like to purchase a tapestry.

ARACHNE: I appreciate your compliments.

CUSTOMER 3: This is the most beautiful weaving I have ever seen!

Greek Myth Plays © 2008 by Carol Pugliano-Martin, Scholastic Teaching Resources

ARACHNE: Well, actually I must agree with you. I am the best weaver in the world.

CUSTOMER 1: And one with a very high opinion of herself!

ARACHNE: I can't help it. It's true.

CUSTOMER 2: The gods have been very good to you to give you such a gift.

ARACHNE: Gods, schmods! The talent is mine. I got this good all by myself.

CUSTOMER 3: Arachne! You should not say such things! Were you not trained by the goddess Athena?

ARACHNE: I suppose. But I'm sure I am a much better weaver even than Athena.

ATHENA: (*Disguised as an old woman*) Would you challenge the goddess Athena to a weaving contest?

CHORUS 1: Don't be foolish, Arachne. No one challenges the gods and wins!

CHORUS 2: Be very careful, Arachne!

ARACHNE: (*To the Choruses*) Oh, be quiet. (*To the woman*) I would challenge Athena. I'm sure she wouldn't stand a chance against me.

ATHENA: (*Revealing herself as Athena*) Then let's do it, you ungrateful girl. I accept your challenge of a weaving contest.

CHORUS 1: Arachne was very surprised to see Athena, but she didn't show it.

CHORUS 2: The crowd stared in awe, wondering what Arachne would do next.

ARACHNE: You're on!

(*Everyone gasps.*)

CHORUS 1: The two weavers began at their looms. Athena wove a bird.

CUSTOMER 1: This bird looks like it could fly right off this tapestry!

CHORUS 2: Arachne wove a flower.

CUSTOMER 2: I can practically smell this flower!

Greek Myth Plays © 2008 by Carol Pugliano-Martin, Scholastic Teaching Resources

CHORUS 1: They wove and wove. Finally they were finished.

CHORUS 2: Athena wove a tapestry that showed the gods in all their glory.

CUSTOMER 3: Arachne, you have woven a tapestry that makes fun of the gods.

CHORUS 1: Arachne, you do not respect the gods!

CHORUS 2: Oh, what will become of you now?!

ATHENA: Arachne, I must admit, you are the better weaver.

ARACHNE: I told you so!

ATHENA: However, your lack of respect for the gods and your pride angers me. I cannot allow it to continue.

CHORUS 1: Athena, what will you do to Arachne?

CHORUS 2: Such a mortal must be punished.

ATHENA: I've got it! Since you love to weave so much, go ahead and continue weaving. But you will do it as a different creature.

CHORUS 1: Athena put a spell on Arachne. Soon Arachne's body shrunk and turned into a black orb. Her limbs turned into eight spindly legs.

(*Everyone gasps.*)

CHORUS 2: A strand of thread curled out of Arachne's mouth. Athena tied the thread to a tree. Arachne was left dangling from a branch.

ATHENA: Your tapestries will still be beautiful, Arachne. But people will hurry to sweep them away!

CHORUS 1: And so ends the tale of Arachne, the first spider.

CHORUS 2: Look for her weaving her beautiful webs and learn what too much pride can do.

ARACHNE: And maybe, just maybe, you won't sweep them away, okay?

THE END

Greek Myth Plays © 2008 by Carol Pugliano-Martin, Scholastic Teaching Resources

Glossary

mortal: a human being

tapestry: a heavy piece of cloth with pictures or patterns woven into it

exquisite: very beautiful and delicate

purchase: buy

Gods, schmods!: slang for "Who cares?" or "Big deal!"

awe: a feeling of admiration and respect, mixed with a little bit of fear

looms: machines used for weaving

orb: sphere, globe, or circle

spindly: long, thin, and rather weak

Greek Myth Plays © 2008 by Carol Pugliano-Martin, Scholastic Teaching Resources

ATALANTA AND THE GREAT RACE

CHARACTERS

Chorus 1
Chorus 2
Servant
King
Queen
Atalanta
(at-uh-LAN-tuh)

Man 1
Man 2
Man 3
Aphrodite
(af-reh-DY-tee)
Hippomenes
(hip-AHM-ih-neez)

CHORUS 1: *(Like a sports announcer)* Ladies and gentlemen, it's time for another great race! Atalanta will race against Hippomenes.

CHORUS 2: If Hippomenes wins, he will get to marry Atalanta. And if Atalanta wins, well, that's another ending. And not a pleasant one for Hippomenes, if you know what we mean.

CHORUS 1: What? You don't know the story of Atalanta and the great race?

CHORUS 2: Well, let's start from the beginning, shall we?

CHORUS 1: It all started when a baby was born to the King of Arcadia.

Greek Myth Plays © 2008 by Carol Pugliano-Martin, Scholastic Teaching Resources

SERVANT: Your highness, the baby has been born.

KING: And is it a son? My greatest wish?

SERVANT: No, your highness. It is a girl child.

KING: A girl? I only want a son. The child must be taken away. Bring me to my wife.

QUEEN: (*Cooing to baby*) Hello, sweet little girl. Hello. I will name you Atalanta.

KING: Give the baby to the servant.

QUEEN: Why?

KING: He must take her away to a mountaintop. Her fate will be up to the gods. A girl can give me nothing. I want a son!

QUEEN: But you can't do that!

KING: I can . . . I will.

CHORUS 2: The servant took the baby away as ordered.

CHORUS 1: But Atalanta did not perish on the mountain.

CHORUS 2: She was found by a mother bear who had two cubs.

CHORUS 1: The bear raised Atalanta as though she too were one of her cubs.

CHORUS 2: Atalanta grew strong in the forest. She learned to climb the tallest trees from her brothers, the cubs.

CHORUS 1: She learned to find food by following the mother bear.

CHORUS 2: But most of all, Atalanta learned to run faster than the wind by racing with the deer of the forest.

ATALANTA: I love my forest home. But I'm curious about the village below. I think I'll take a trip down there.

CHORUS 1: Atalanta entered the village and walked around. Soon the people began to notice her.

Greek Myth Plays © 2008 by Carol Pugliano-Martin, Scholastic Teaching Resources

MAN 1:	Hey, check out the new girl!
MAN 2:	She's beautiful!
MAN 3:	I'd give anything to marry her!
CHORUS 2:	Even your life?
MEN:	Huh?
CHORUS 1:	You'll see.
CHORUS 2:	Word got to the king about the strange new girl.
KING:	A girl who lives on the mountain?
SERVANT:	Yes. It is said she was raised by a family of bears.
KING:	That must be Atalanta, my long-lost daughter! Bring her to me for I must apologize for what I did.
CHORUS 1:	The servant brought Atalanta to the king.
ATALANTA:	You wanted to see me?
KING:	Yes. For you are my daughter, and I beg your forgiveness for leaving you on the mountain.
ATALANTA:	Why should I forgive you?
KING:	I am old. I am alone now. My poor wife has died, and we had no more children. Please, I beg of you.
ATALANTA:	Oh, all right. But you must promise that there will be no hunting in the forest, for the animals are my real family.
KING:	Done. Thank you. And now, as princess, you must be wed.
ATALANTA:	Wed? I want no man!
KING:	But a princess must have a husband!
ATALANTA:	I will wed on one condition. Whoever can beat me in a race will become my husband. But whoever loses will die.

Greek Myth Plays © 2008 by Carol Pugliano-Martin, Scholastic Teaching Resources

KING: Ouch. That's harsh.

ATALANTA: You left me on a mountain when I was a baby, and you're saying I'm harsh?

KING: Touché! *(too-SHAY)*

CHORUS 2: So many men jumped at the chance to race Atalanta, even though they knew the terrible risk.

CHORUS 1: *(As announcer)* And now, the first runner will try to beat Atalanta.

CHORUS 2: On your marks, get set, go!

CHORUS 1: Atalanta wins easily.

MAN 2: *(To Man 1)* Oooh. Tough luck, chum.

CHORUS 2: And now, for the second race. On your marks, get set, go!

CHORUS 1: Again, Atalanta wins without effort.

MAN 3: *(To Man 2)* Bye-bye, now!

CHORUS 2: Next victim . . . er, racer. On your marks, get set, go!

CHORUS 1: Surprise, surprise . . . Atalanta wins again.

MAN 3: Yikes!

ATALANTA: *(To King)* You see, father, I will not marry, for no man can beat me.

CHORUS 2: The King shakes his head sadly as he and Atalanta head back to the palace.

CHORUS 1: Meanwhile, Hippomenes, a handsome mortal, and Aphrodite, the goddess of love, were cooking up a scheme.

HIPPOMENES: Atalanta is so beautiful and smart. I must win her hand. But she is too fast a runner for me to beat.

Greek Myth Plays © 2008 by Carol Pugliano-Martin, Scholastic Teaching Resources

APHRODITE: Hippomenes, I like you. And I love to see mortals in love and married. I have a plan to make you win. (*Handing three apples to Hippomenes*) Take these golden apples. Three times during the race, throw them in front of Atalanta. She will stop to pick them up, and you will win.

HIPPOMENES: But what if she doesn't pick them up?

APHRODITE: Would the goddess of love steer you wrong? Trust me, she will be unable to resist them!

HIPPOMENES: Thank you, Aphrodite! I'll do it!

CHORUS 2: As Hippomenes gets ready for the race, Atalanta is having second thoughts.

ATALANTA: I won't do it!

KING: But why not? Are you afraid you'll lose?

ATALANTA: No. I am afraid I'll win. And Hippomenes is such a good man. Cute, too.

KING: A deal's a deal. You will race.

CHORUS 1: Hippomenes double checks to make sure the golden apples are hidden in his tunic. He and Atalanta line up to race.

CHORUS 2: On your marks, get set, go!

CHORUS 1: (*As announcer*) The two runners are neck and neck. But look! Atalanta is pulling ahead.

CHORUS 2: (*As announcer*) What's this? Hippomenes has thrown a golden apple in front of Atalanta. She's stopping to pick it up! She looks like she's under a spell!

ATALANTA: Oooh!

CHORUS 1: Hippomenes is speeding ahead!

CHORUS 2: But wait! Here comes Atalanta again. She's in the lead!

CHORUS 1: Another golden apple is thrown.

Greek Myth Plays © 2008 by Carol Pugliano-Martin, Scholastic Teaching Resources

ATALANTA: (*Like a zombie*) Shiny!

CHORUS 2: And Hippomenes is back in the lead!

ATALANTA: (*Snapping out of the trance*) Those darned apples are so beautiful. I can't resist them! But I must win.

CHORUS 1: Atalanta is in the lead once again. She is sure to win.

HIPPOMENES: (*To Atalanta*) One last apple and the chance to save my life and win your love!

CHORUS 2: There goes another apple. And there goes Atalanta again.

ATALANTA: (*Back in a trance*) Pretty apple!

CHORUS 1: And the winner is . . . Hippomenes!

HIPPOMENES: Atalanta, will you marry me?

ATALANTA: (*Back to normal*) I will.

CHORUS 2: The King places Atalanta's hand in Hippomenes's, and they are wed.

CHORUS 1: So that's where the story ends, right?

CHORUS 2: Wrong! You see, the two lovers forgot to thank Aphrodite for her help. They were turned into lions, but they still lived and loved happily ever after.

ATALANTA AND HIPPOMENES: ROAR!

APHRODITE: (*To audience*) Don't mess with the goddess of love!

THE END

Greek Myth Plays © 2008 by Carol Pugliano-Martin, Scholastic Teaching Resources

Glossary

highness: a title of honor for royalty

fate: the force that some people believe controls events and decides what happens to people

perish: to die, or to be destroyed

condition: something that is needed before another thing can happen or be allowed

harsh: cruel or rough

touché: used to acknowledge a point well made by an opponent in an argument

chum: a friend, buddy, or pal

mortal: a human being

scheme: a plan or plot for doing something

steer: to guide or to direct

tunic: a loose, sleeveless garment

trance: a conscious state in which you are not fully aware of what is happening around you

Greek Myth Plays © 2008 by Carol Pugliano-Martin, Scholastic Teaching Resources

DAEDALUS AND ICARUS

CHARACTERS

KING MINOS
(MY-nahs)
SERVANT
CHORUS 1
CHORUS 2
DAEDALUS
(DED-uh-lus)

ICARUS (IK-uh-rus)
ARIADNE
(ar-ee-AD-nee)
THESEUS
(THEE-see-us)
RED BIRD
YELLOW BIRD

CHORUS 1: Daedalus was a master builder who lived with his son Icarus in Athens.

CHORUS 2: King Minos ruled the kingdom of Crete. One day he decided to make some changes in his kingdom.

KING MINOS: I need a new building in my kingdom. Something tall. Something grand. Like me! But who can build it? I'm tired of the local builders.

SERVANT: Why don't you get Daedalus from Athens? After all, he designed your maze.

KING MINOS: Yes. He did a great job with that. Each year I sacrifice some poor souls by putting them in that maze with the man-eating Minotaur, the bull. No one ever gets out. I will send for Daedalus.

Greek Myth Plays © 2008 by Carol Pugliano-Martin, Scholastic Teaching Resources

CHORUS 1:	So Daedalus and his son, Icarus, traveled to Crete. Daedalus would now build for King Minos.
CHORUS 2:	Soon it was time for King Minos's yearly sacrifice in the maze. The king happened to choose Daedalus's cousin Theseus to sacrifice to the Minotaur.
DAEDALUS:	So, poor Theseus has been chosen.
ICARUS:	Father, isn't there anything you can do?
DAEDALUS:	I don't think so. I made that maze so well, I don't think there's any hope.
CHORUS 1:	The king's daughter, Ariadne, also did not want Theseus to be a victim of the maze.
CHORUS 2:	She had seen Theseus and fallen in love with him at first sight.
ARIADNE:	Daedalus, I beg of you, don't let Theseus perish in the maze. You designed it. Surely you can find a way out for him!
DAEDALUS:	(*Thinking aloud*) Well, there might be one way . . .
CHORUS 1:	Daedalus visited Theseus in his prison cell the night before the sacrifice was to take place.
DAEDALUS:	There is a small tunnel that leads outside the maze. It is there to deliver food to the Minotaur. It is quite tiny, so you'll have to squeeze through.
THESEUS:	I can do it, Daedalus. For I have eaten next to nothing here in prison. I am now quite thin and can fit in a tight place.
DAEDALUS:	(*Handing a map to Theseus*) Here, study this map. These are the plans I used to design the maze. The tunnel is here. You must distract the Minotaur and then move quickly.
THESEUS:	I will, cousin. Thank you so much.
CHORUS 2:	The next day, Theseus was put in the maze. Ariadne was instructed by Daedalus to wait outside the tunnel. When Theseus got out, he and Ariadne would run away together.

Greek Myth Plays © 2008 by Carol Pugliano-Martin, Scholastic Teaching Resources

CHORUS 1: The Minotaur went after Theseus immediately. Seeing that he was near the tunnel, Theseus threw a rock past the bull. Thinking it was another victim, the bull turned and ran the other way. Theseus scurried through the tiny tunnel and escaped with Ariadne.

CHORUS 2: King Minos was not pleased about these events. He called for Daedalus and Icarus.

KING MINOS: Daedalus, only you could have helped Theseus escape. You are the only person who knows the inside of the maze. Now my daughter is gone. As punishment, you and your son Icarus will be imprisoned in my tower forever.

ICARUS: Nice going, Dad.

DAEDALUS: Relax, I'll think of something.

CHORUS 1: Daedalus and Icarus were put in the tower. Each day they were visited by several birds who flew by to say hello.

ICARUS: Look at those birds, father. Oh, if we only had wings and could fly out of this tower and away forever.

DAEDALUS: That's it!

CHORUS 2: Suddenly a beautiful red bird flew to the tower bars.

RED BIRD: Hello, Daedalus. Hello, Icarus. It's good to see you both today.

DAEDALUS: Hello, red bird. May I ask a favor? Could you please give my son and me a beautiful red feather each?

RED BIRD: Of course. I have so many. I can do without two.

CHORUS 1: And the red bird gave Daedalus two red feathers.

CHORUS 2: Later a yellow bird flew by.

DAEDALUS: Yellow bird, may I please have two of your beautiful feathers?

YELLOW BIRD: Certainly. I'm flattered that you like them. (*Hands two feathers to Daedalus*)

Greek Myth Plays © 2008 by Carol Pugliano-Martin, Scholastic Teaching Resources

CHORUS 1:   Next came a blue bird, a green bird, and several other beautifully colored birds.

CHORUS 2:   Daedalus got feathers from all of them.

ICARUS: What's up with the feathers, Dad?

DAEDALUS: You wanted wings, and you shall have wings. My son, we will fly out of this tower!

CHORUS 1:   Daedalus got to work. He made two beautiful sets of wings, one for himself and one for Icarus.

DAEDALUS: (*Handing Icarus a set of wings made from the birds' feathers*) Icarus, put these on. We will be like beautiful rainbows soaring in the sky.

ICARUS: Cool!

DAEDALUS: You must be very careful. Do not fly too close to the ocean. Your wings will get wet and fall off. Do not fly too close to the sun. The heat will melt the wax that holds your wings together and you will perish.

CHORUS 2:   But Icarus wasn't paying attention to Daedalus. He was too excited about the wings.

DAEDALUS: When I count to three, jump out of the window and start flapping. One, two, three . . .

CHORUS 1:   Away went Daedalus and Icarus. Just like Daedalus had said, they looked like two beautiful rainbows in the sky.

ICARUS: Weee! This is great! Look at me!

DAEDALUS: Not too high, Icarus! Remember the sun!

ICARUS: I'll be fine. Look, I am flying even higher than the birds!

DAEDALUS: Fly lower, Icarus. Come closer to me right now.

CHORUS 2:   But Icarus did not listen. He flew close to the sun. His wings melted, and he fell into the ocean and was never seen again.

DAEDALUS: My son!

Greek Myth Plays © 2008 by Carol Pugliano-Martin, Scholastic Teaching Resources

ICARUS:	Bummer!
CHORUS 1:	Daedalus was terribly sad. But he knew he must fly on to his freedom. He settled in another land, a free man.
CHORUS 2:	And to this day, the water that Icarus fell in is known as the Icarian Sea.
ICARUS:	Cool!

THE END

Glossary

sacrifice: to offer something to God or a god

maze: a complicated network of paths or lines, made as a puzzle to find your way through

perish: to die, or to be destroyed

distract: to direct someone's attention elsewhere

scurried: hurried, or ran with short, quick steps

flattered: complimented

Greek Myth Plays © 2008 by Carol Pugliano-Martin, Scholastic Teaching Resources

KING MIDAS AND THE GOLDEN TOUCH

Greek Myth Plays © 2008 by Carol Pugliano-Martin, Scholastic Teaching Resources

CHARACTERS

CHORUS 1   DIONYSUS
CHORUS 2   (dy-uh-NY-suhs)
KING MIDAS (MY-das)   MIDAS'S SERVANT
GRAPE PICKER 1   MIDAS'S WIFE
GRAPE PICKER 2   MIDAS'S CHILD

CHORUS 1: Once there was a king named Midas. Like most kings, he was very wealthy.

CHORUS 2: But Midas was not satisfied with his wealth. Like many kings, he wanted more wealth.

MIDAS: Gold, gold, wonderful gold!
Whenever I see it, I never feel old.
There's one special thing that will make me feel glad—
That's to have the most gold a mortal's ever had!

CHORUS 1:	One day some grape pickers found a satyr (*SAY-tuhr*) asleep in Midas's field.
CHORUS 2:	A satyr is half man and half goat, and this one was lying in the king's favorite flower bed near a stream.
GRAPE PICKER 1:	Be on your way, satyr!
GRAPE PICKER 2:	He's sound asleep. He won't budge!
GRAPE PICKER 1:	Well, we have to get him away from here, or Midas might be mad!
GRAPE PICKER 2:	Hmm . . . there must be something we can do.
MIDAS:	Do about what?
GRAPE PICKER 1:	This satyr, your majesty.
GRAPE PICKER 2:	He's in your favorite flower bed.
MIDAS:	That's no matter. Let him be. The poor creature must need his rest if he's sleeping so soundly.
GRAPE PICKERS 1 & 2:	Yes, your majesty.
CHORUS 1:	So the grape pickers left as the satyr slept on.
CHORUS 2:	Suddenly, Dionysus, the god of wine appeared.
DIONYSUS:	Well done, Midas!
MIDAS:	(*Bowing*) Dionysus, what brings you to my vineyard?
DIONYSUS:	I have seen the work of kindness you have bestowed upon my friend. For that you will be rewarded. What is your wish?
MIDAS:	My wish? I wish for gold, gold, wonderful gold! Whenever I see it I never feel old. There's one special thing that will make me feel glad— That's to have the most gold a mortal's ever had! I wish that everything I touch would turn to gold!

Greek Myth Plays © 2008 by Carol Pugliano-Martin, Scholastic Teaching Resources

CHORUS 1 & 2: Be careful what you wish for, Midas!

MIDAS: Shush!

DIONYSUS: But you already have more gold than any mortal could ever need!

MIDAS: Ah, there can never be enough gold! May I have my wish?

DIONYSUS: If that is your wish, then it is granted. Now everything you touch will turn to gold.

MIDAS: Thank you, kind Dionysus!

CHORUS 1: After Dionysus and the satyr had left, Midas ran through his gardens, testing his wish.

CHORUS 2: As his feet ran on the grass, it turned to gold!

CHORUS 1: He touched the swaying branches of his trees. The trees turned to gold!

CHORUS 2: And each rosebush he touched turned to gold!

MIDAS: Hee, hee! Hah, hah! Hoo, hoo!

CHORUS 1: Midas was ecstatic.

CHORUS 2: Midas's servant entered, carrying a glass.

SERVANT: Your majesty, I have brought you a cool drink.

MIDAS: Wonderful. Thank you so much.

CHORUS 1: As Midas put his hand on the servant's shoulder, the servant froze and turned to gold!

MIDAS: Oh, my!

CHORUS 2: In came Midas's dog, barking happily and nuzzling up to Midas. She, too, turned to gold!

MIDAS: Oh, dear!

CHORUS 1: Midas's wife entered with her arms extended to embrace Midas.

Greek Myth Plays © 2003 by Carol Pugliano-Martin, Scholastic Teaching Resources

WIFE: Darling, I've been looking all over for you!

MIDAS: Stay back! Do not touch me!

WIFE: What on earth is going on?

MIDAS: It's a long story. Just stay away.

CHORUS 2: Whew! That was close! Oh, no! Here comes his child!

CHILD: Daddy, daddy!

MIDAS: No, my child. No!

CHORUS 1: But it was too late. Midas's child embraced Midas and instantly turned to gold.

MIDAS: (*To the sky*) Oh, Dionysus! Rid me of this terrible wish!

DIONYSUS: But you have more gold than any mortal. And you will have even more!

MIDAS: My child. My precious child. Nothing is more important!

DIONYSUS: (*Handing Midas a large jar*) Very well. Take this amphora. Bring it to the river and fill it with water. Pour it over everything that has turned to gold, and it will be undone.

MIDAS: (*Taking the jar*) Oh, thank you, kind god.

DIONYSUS: You're welcome. And Midas?

MIDAS: Yes?

DIONYSUS: Next time, be careful what you wish for.

CHORUS 1 & 2: Told you so!

MIDAS: Oh, shush!

CHORUS 2: So Midas did as Dionysus said, and everything that had turned to gold was turned back.

SERVANT: I'll get you some bread to go with your drink.

Greek Myth Plays © 2008 by Carol Pugliano-Martin, Scholastic Teaching Resources

CHILD:	Daddy, daddy! Come play with me!
MIDAS:	(*Hugging his child*) Yes, my dear child. Yes!

(*To audience*)

Ladies and gentlemen, take it from me.
Some wishes are bad, as you can see.
I've learned my lesson and now I confess
All I need is what I already possess.

CHORUS 1 & 2:	Told you so!
MIDAS:	Oh, shush!

THE END

Glossary

mortal: a human being

satyr: a mythological creature that is often shown as having the ears, horns, and legs of a goat and the rest of its body as human

budge: to move or shift

bestowed: gave someone a gift or prize

granted: given

swaying: moving or swinging from side to side

ecstatic: feeling great happiness or extreme joy

nuzzling: cuddling close to someone

embrace: hug

rid: to remove something that is unwanted

precious: very special or dear

amphora: an ancient Greek jar with two handles and a narrow neck

confess: to admit that you have done something wrong

possess: to own

Greek Myth Plays © 2008 by Carol Pugliano-Martin, Scholastic Teaching Resources

THE TROJAN HORSE

CHARACTERS

CHORUS 1	ODYSSEUS
CHORUS 2	(oh-DIS-ee-us)
PRINCE	GREEK 1
DUKE	GREEK 2
KING	GREEK 3
HELEN (HEL-en)	TROJAN 1
KING MENELAUS	TROJAN 2
(men-uh-LAY-us)	TROJAN 3
PARIS (PAR-is)	

CHORUS 1: Once there was a woman named Helen, who was the most beautiful woman in all the world.

CHORUS 2: Every man in the land wished to wed Helen.

PRINCE: What a divine goddess. If only she were mine.

DUKE: Step aside, Princey. If Helen will be anyone's, she will be mine.

KING: Tough luck, chums. Surely Helen would prefer a king!

HELEN: It isn't easy to be me!

CHORUS 1: Helen did eventually choose a king to marry. King Menelaus of Greece became the husband of the beautiful Helen and the envy of every man around.

Greek Myth Plays © 2008 by Carol Pugliano-Martin, Scholastic Teaching Resources

CHORUS 2:	But there was one man, Paris from Troy, who would not give up on winning Helen, even after she was married.
PARIS:	I will win Helen's love. I must! (*Calling Helen*) Helen! Oh, Helen!
HELEN:	Yes, who's there?
PARIS:	I am Paris from Troy. Please come away with me to Troy. Surely you are not happy with King Menelaus, for he is old and tired while I am young and strong.
HELEN:	No, I love my husband. I cannot leave him to be with you. (*She turns away*)
PARIS:	(*To audience*) I must have Helen. Okay, if she won't go with me willingly, then I have no choice.
CHORUS 1:	Paris stole Helen away from her home and brought her to Troy.
HELEN:	Help! Help!
CHORUS 2:	King Menelaus was heartbroken.
KING MENELAUS:	Woe is me! My beloved Helen has been taken from me. Whatever will I do? Now I am alone. Boo, hoo!
GREEK 1:	Hey, what's this whining, King? You are a powerful man, handsome, brave, and wise.
GREEK 2:	He's right. Enough crying. You must fight to get Helen back.
GREEK 3:	Yes! And we will help you. We'll go to war to take Helen back!
CHORUS 1:	And the Greeks did go to war. The war between the Greeks and the Trojans lasted for ten years with no outcome.
HELEN:	All this over little ol' me?
CHORUS 2:	The Greeks knew they had to come up with something new. And they knew just the man to do it: young Odysseus.
ODYSSEUS:	King Menelaus, I have an idea. It's a bit unusual, but I hope you will indulge me by listening to me and considering my plan.

Greek Myth Plays © 2008 by Carol Pugliano-Martin, Scholastic Teaching Resources

CHORUS 1: Odysseus told the King and his court his plan.

GREEK 1: That's ridiculous!

GREEK 2: It will never work.

GREEK 3: A wooden horse indeed!

KING MENELAUS: Enough! Odysseus, I'll admit you have a strange plan, but since nothing else has worked, I think we will try it.

ODYSSEUS: Thank you, your majesty. Let's get to work!

CHORUS 2: The Greeks got to work, building a giant wooden horse that they would offer to the Trojans as a peace offering. The Greeks would also pretend to sail away from Troy.

CHORUS 1: But in reality, the Greeks would hide inside the horse and attack the Trojans when they were asleep.

CHORUS 2: Finally, they were done building the horse. Some Greeks pulled the giant horse to the gates of Troy and hid inside.

TROJAN 1: What is this? A giant wooden horse?

TROJAN 2: (*Taking the note from the horse and reading it*) Here's a note: Dear Trojans, we give up. You win. Here's a gift for you to help make things right between us.

TROJAN 3: Hah! Those cowards! Still, it's a nice horse and will look great within our walls. Come help me pull it through the gates so we can show Paris.

CHORUS 1: Meanwhile, the Greeks were getting impatient inside the horse.

GREEK 1: It worked! We're going in!

GREEK 2: Good thing. I'm hot and cranky.

GREEK 3: Well, sit tight and be quiet! It won't be long now!

CHORUS 2: The Greeks stayed still until nightfall. Then, when the Trojans went to sleep, the Greeks jumped out of the horse, and that was the end of Troy.

Greek Myth Plays © 2008 by Carol Pugliano-Martin, Scholastic Teaching Resources

CHORUS 1:	The Greeks grabbed Helen and brought her back to King Menelaus.
CHORUS 2:	And they lived happily ever after.
HELEN:	Beauty sure has its price!

THE END

Glossary

wed: to get married to someone

chums: friends, buddies, or pals

envy: the wish that you could have something that another person has or do something that he or she has done

willingly: doing something readily and eagerly

woe: great sadness or grief; sorrow; suffering

outcome: result

indulge: to let someone have his or her own way

coward: someone who is easily scared and runs away from frightening situations

cranky: acting in an annoyed way; grouchy

nightfall: the period of time at dusk when the light of day is ending and night begins

Greek Myth Plays © 2008 by Carol Pugliano-Martin, Scholastic Teaching Resources